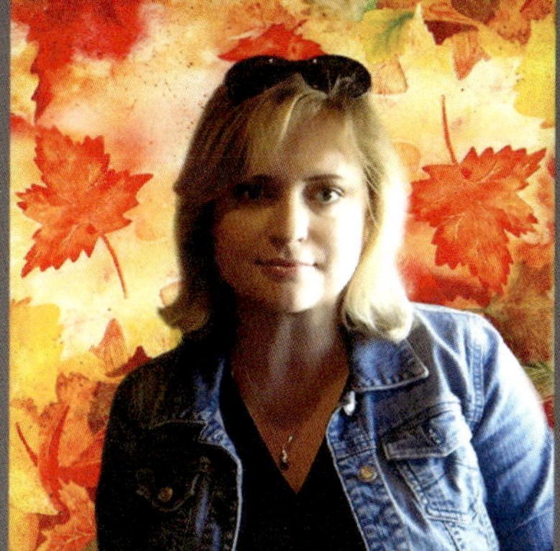

About The Artist

Irina is an award winning artist and illustrator. Her art has been published in Best Of Artists - Watermedia - Volume II, Somatic Psychotherapy Today magazine, Spirit Seeker magazine, and People magazine online. Her illustrated sketchbooks Travel With Me, Down My Street, and Travelogy are on diplay of the NY Public Library.

She won her first award at age 15 during the Junior Art Show in St. Petersburg, Russia. Since then, she has been recognized by numerous organizations and galleries. A few years ago, Irina became an American Art Award Winner in Realism category.
Her passion is painting with watercolors, her main style is contemporary realism and yet the abstract paintings and decorative designs are not left behind.

Most of Irina Sztukowski's original paintings are in private collections throughout the world. To name a few locations, besides the U.S., her artworks are presented in Australia, Canada, Great Britain, Netherlands, Russia, and Spain.

She is a proud member of AWS -American Watercolor Society and a Life Member of TWSA -Transparent Watercolor Society of America. She was also happy to serve the community as the director of the Outreach Program for CWA -California Watercolor Association.

Before coming to the US, she studied art in the St.Petersburg Academy of Art, the Art-Industrial College in St. Petersburg, Russia. She received Bachelor of Arts from The Academy of Culture. While in Russia she was a successful artist selling her works. She continued her journey through the art world after coming to the U.S., resulting in her exploring the creative process. Even though Irina is an accomplished artist she never stops learning as much as she can about the arts. As the result of that eagerness she earned Fine Art degree while in America. These days, Irina Sztukowski continues showing her paintings in local galleries, in the galleries throughout the U.S. and business offices.

Table of Contents

1. Around the world...........................1
2. California..5
3. Colors of Russia.............................9
4. Down my Street...............................13

Around The World

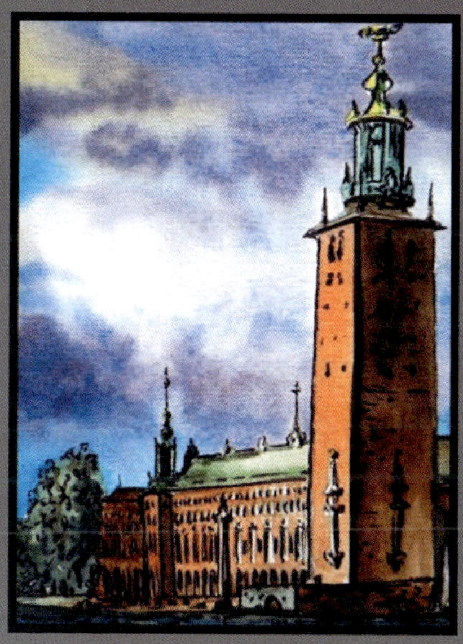

Stadshus,
Sockholm, Sweden

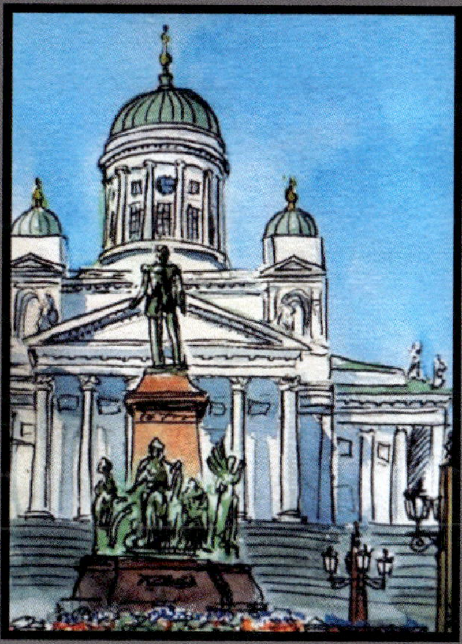

Lutheran Cathedral,
Helsinki, Finland

Around The World

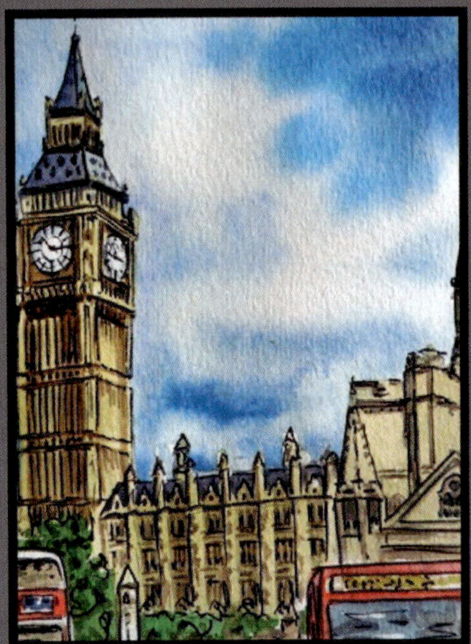

Big Ben Tower,
London, United Kingdom

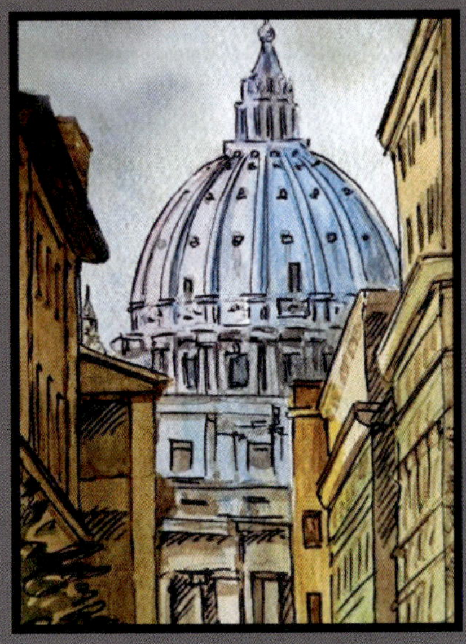

Vatican

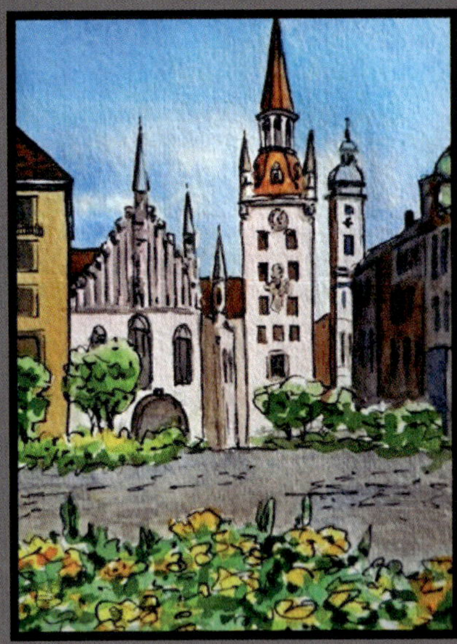

Marienplatz,
Munich, Germany

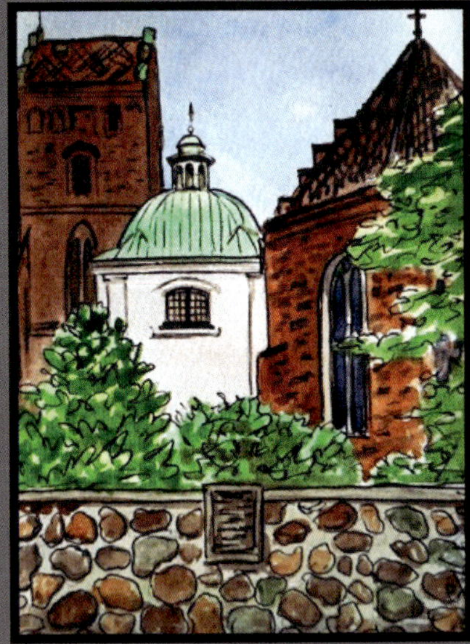

Church of Virgin Mary,
Warsaw, Poland

Around The World

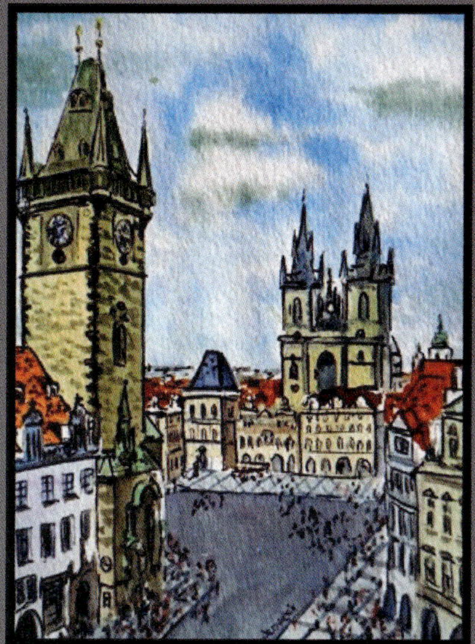

Old Town Square,
Prague, Czech Republic

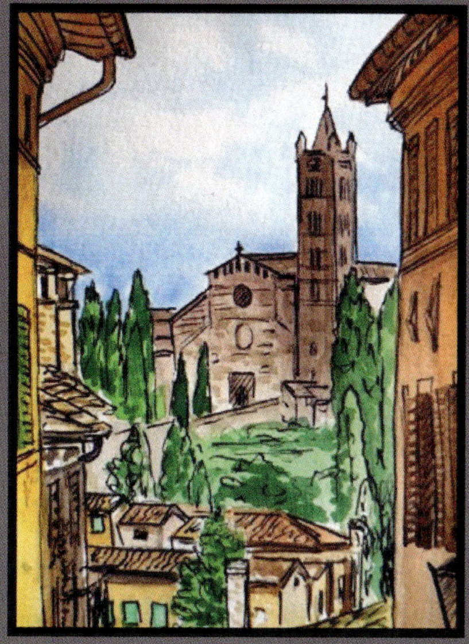

Siena, Italy

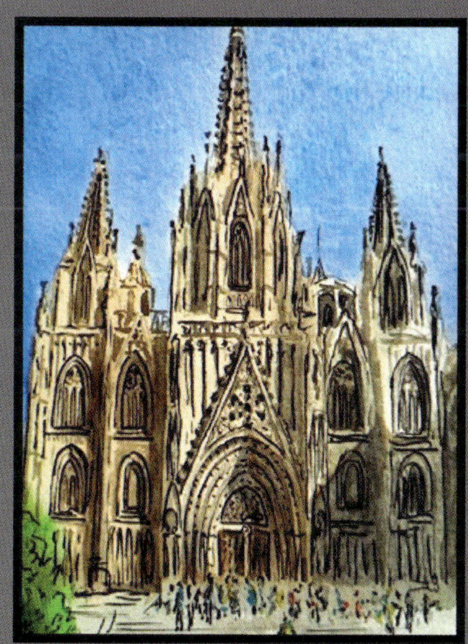

Cathedral of Barcelona,
Barcelona, Spain

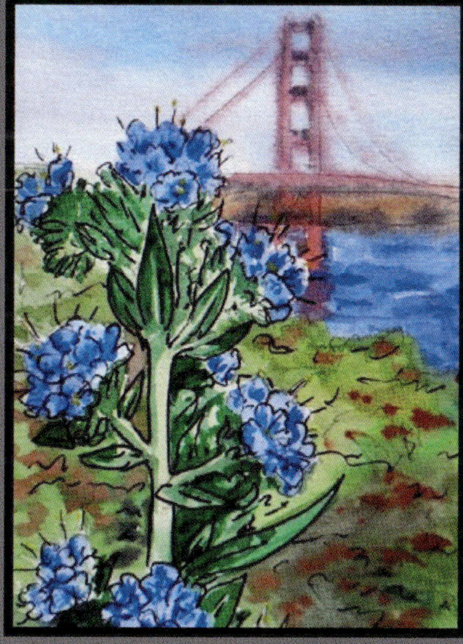

Golden Gate Bridge,
San Francisco, California,
United States of America

Around The World

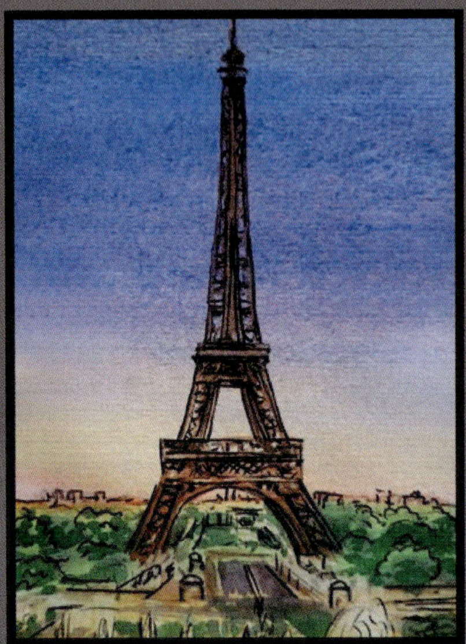

Effel Tower,
Paris, France

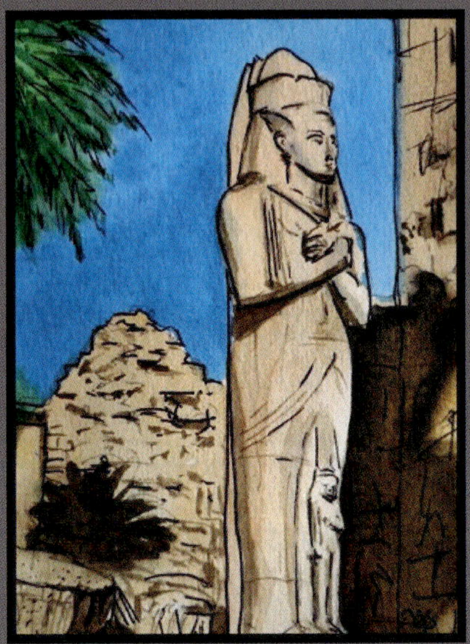

Karnak Temple,
Luxor, Egypt

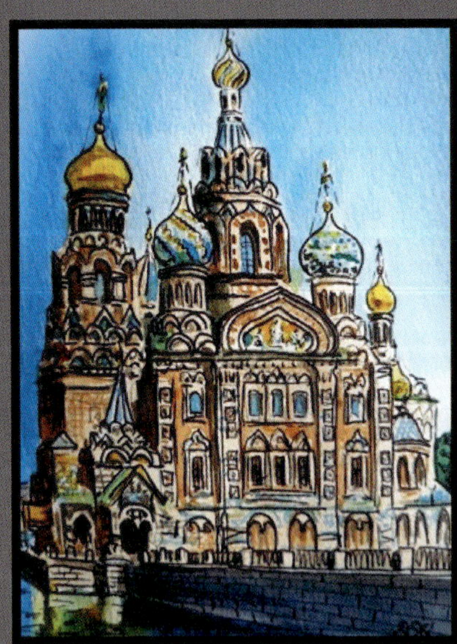

Church of the Savior on Blood,
Saint Petersburg, Russia

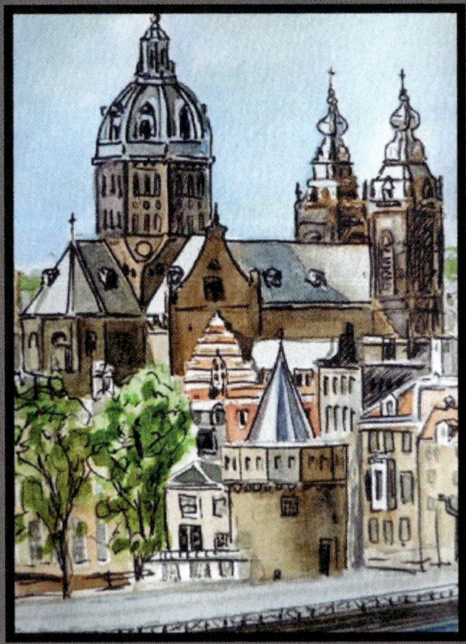

Church of St Nicholas,
Amsterdam, Netherlands

California

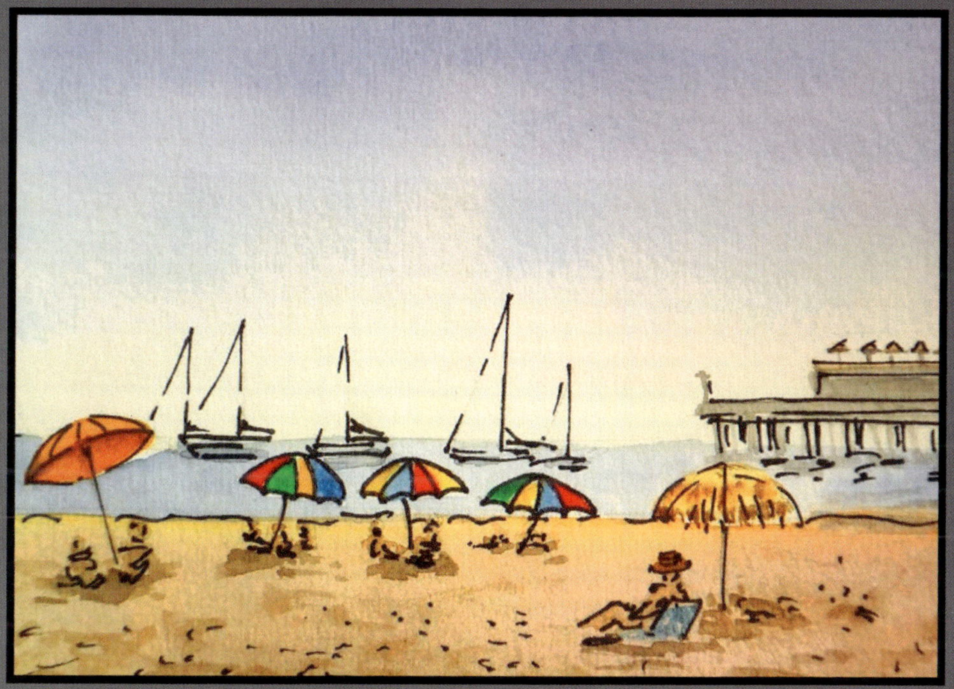

Capitola

California

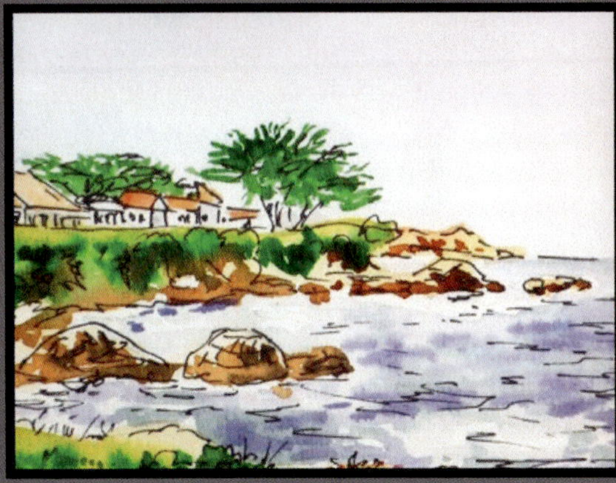

Monterey

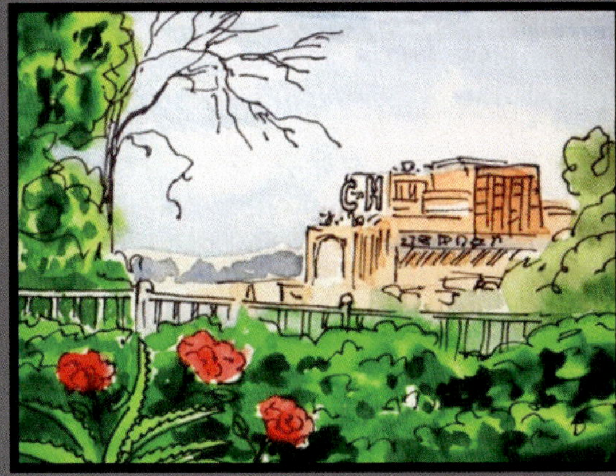

Crockett

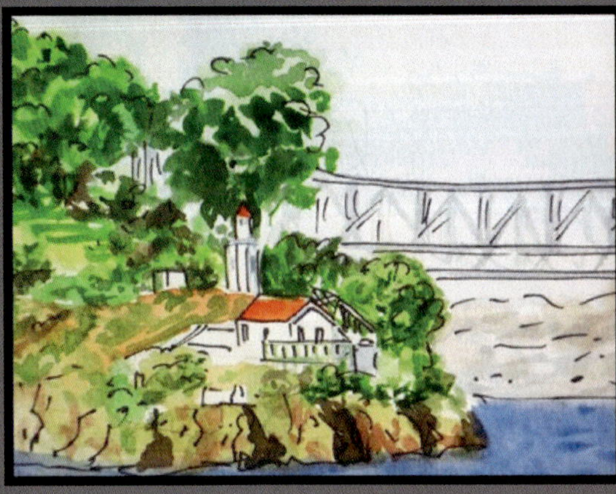

Treasure Island

California

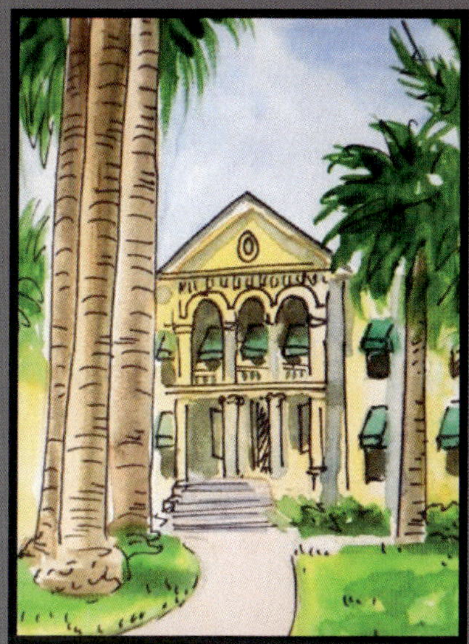

Hanford

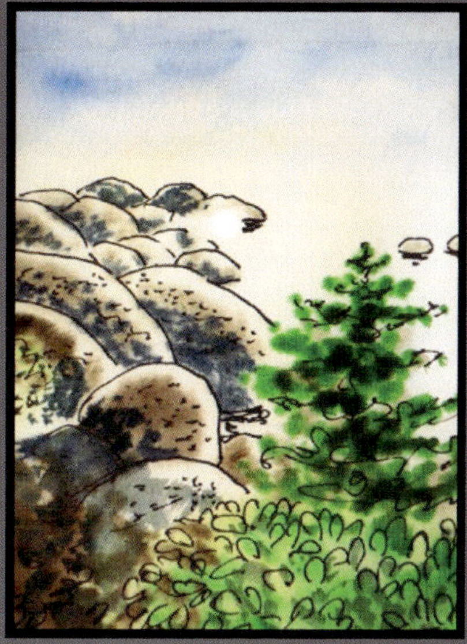

Lake Tahoe

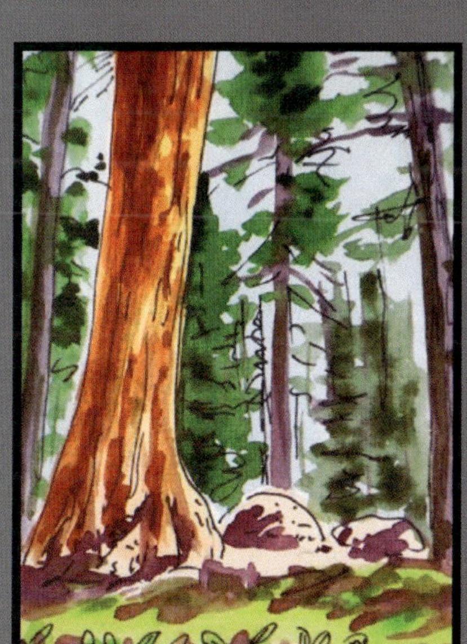

Sequoia National Park

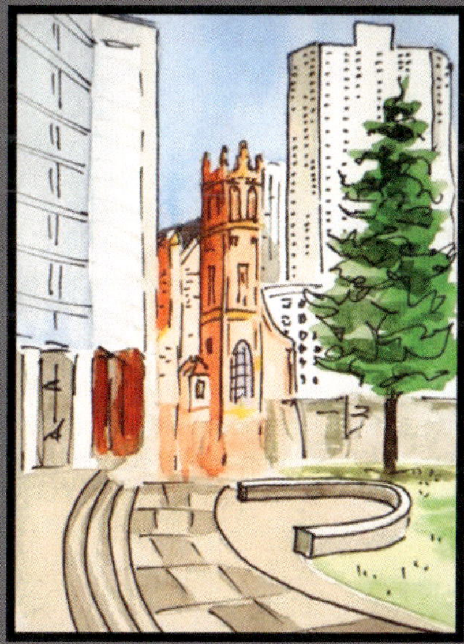

San Francisco

California

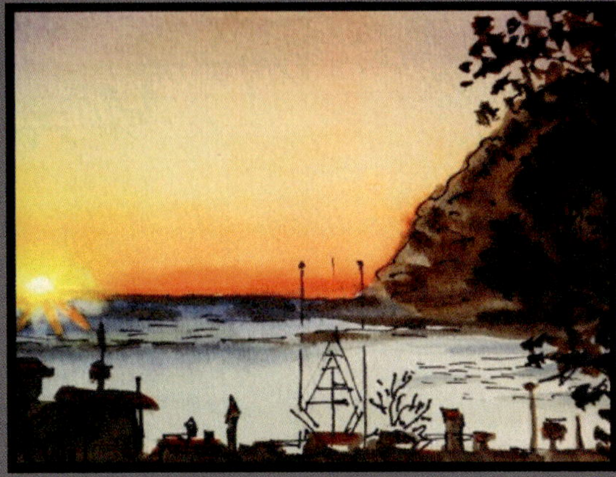

Morro Bay

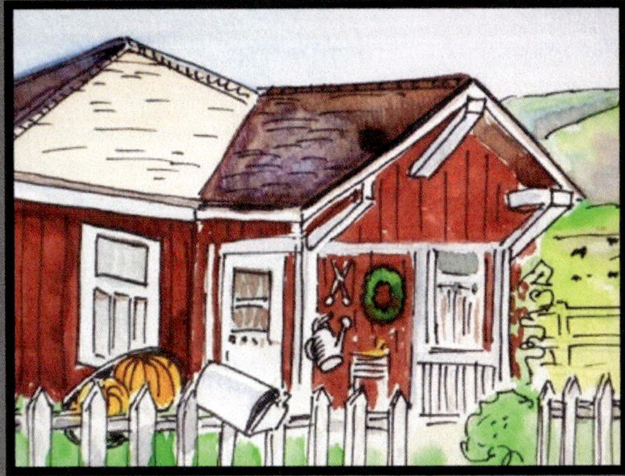

Harmony

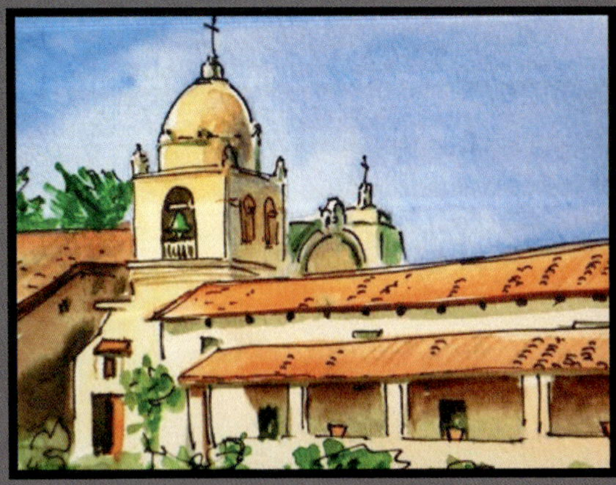

Carmel

Colors of Russia

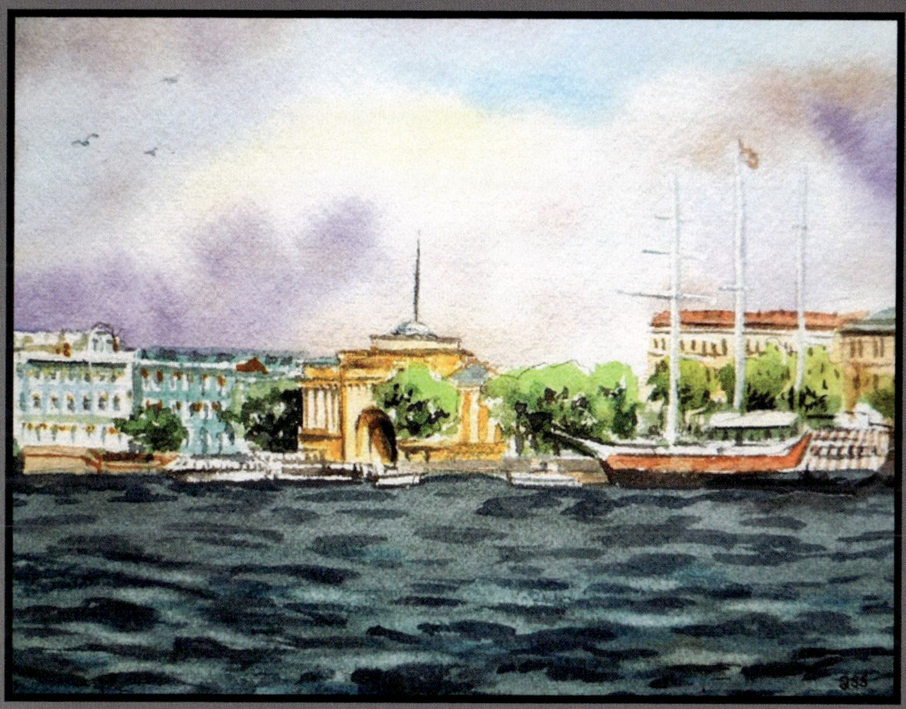

Neva River, Saint Petersburg, Russia

Colors of Russia

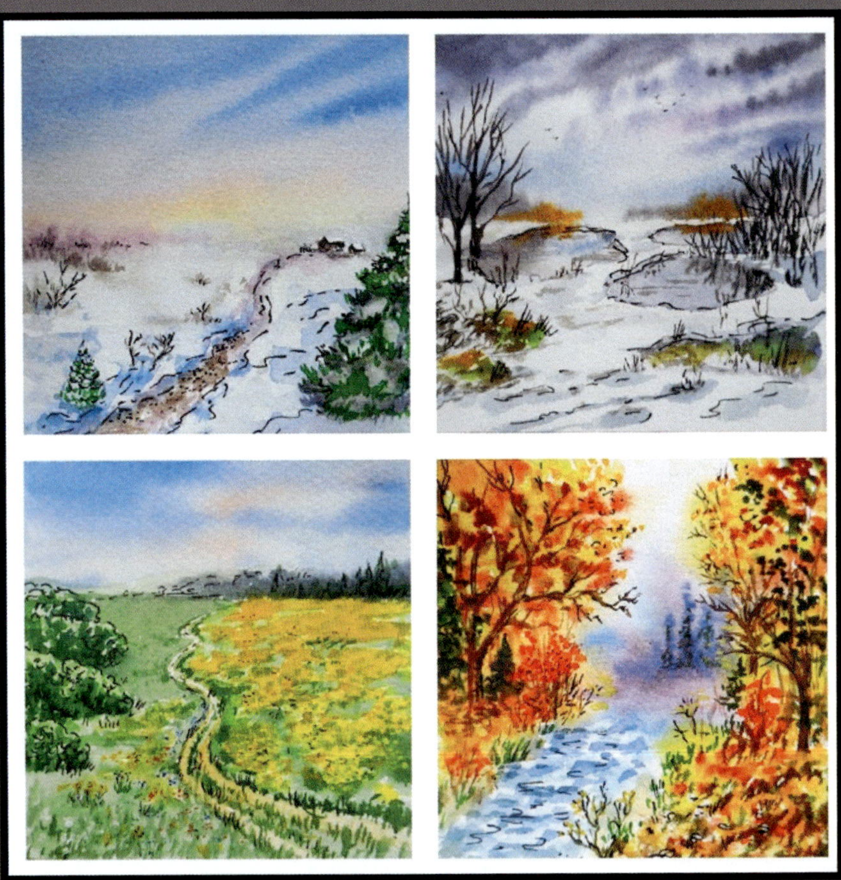

Seasons

Colors of Russia

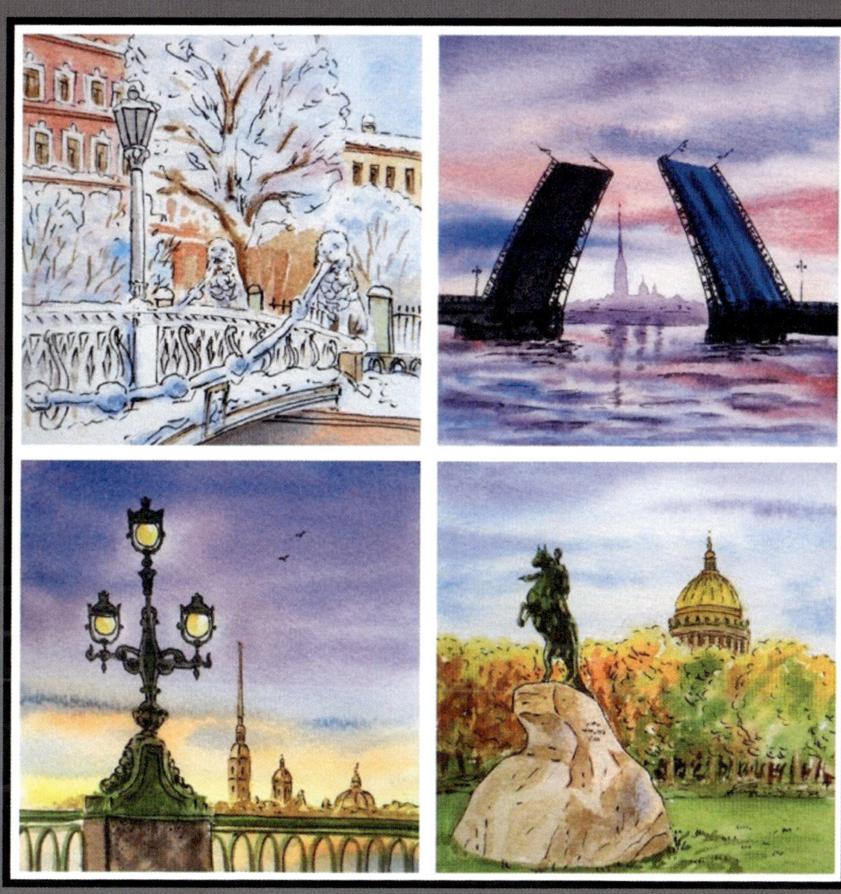

Saint Petersburg, Russia

Colors of Russia

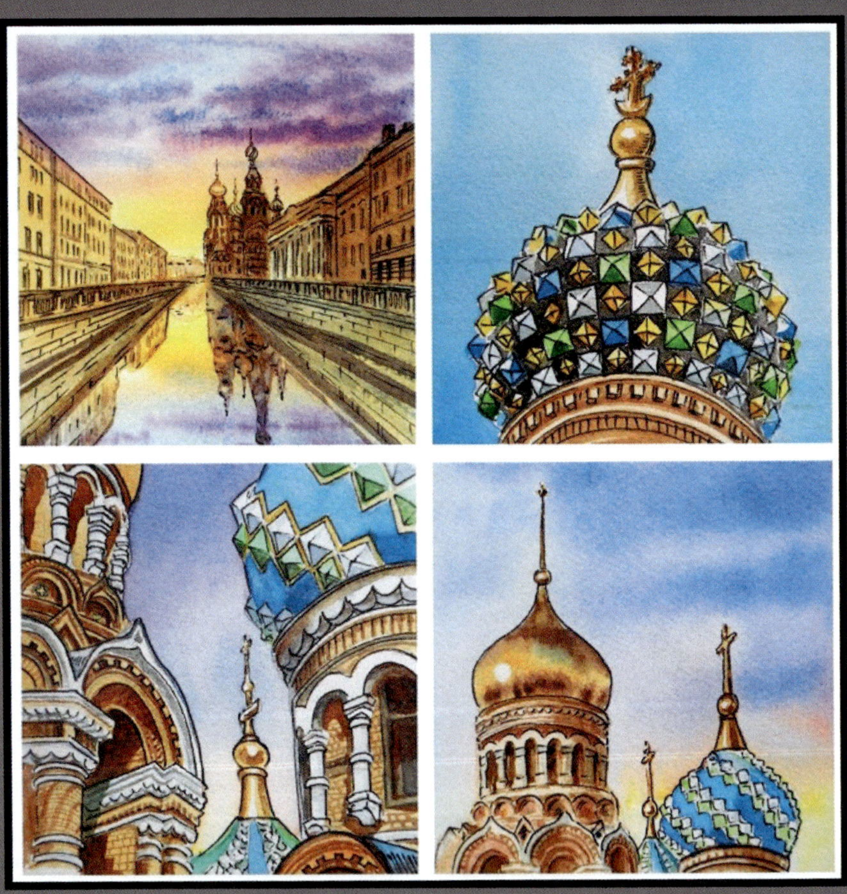

Church of the Savior on Blood, Saint Petersburg, Russia

Down My Street

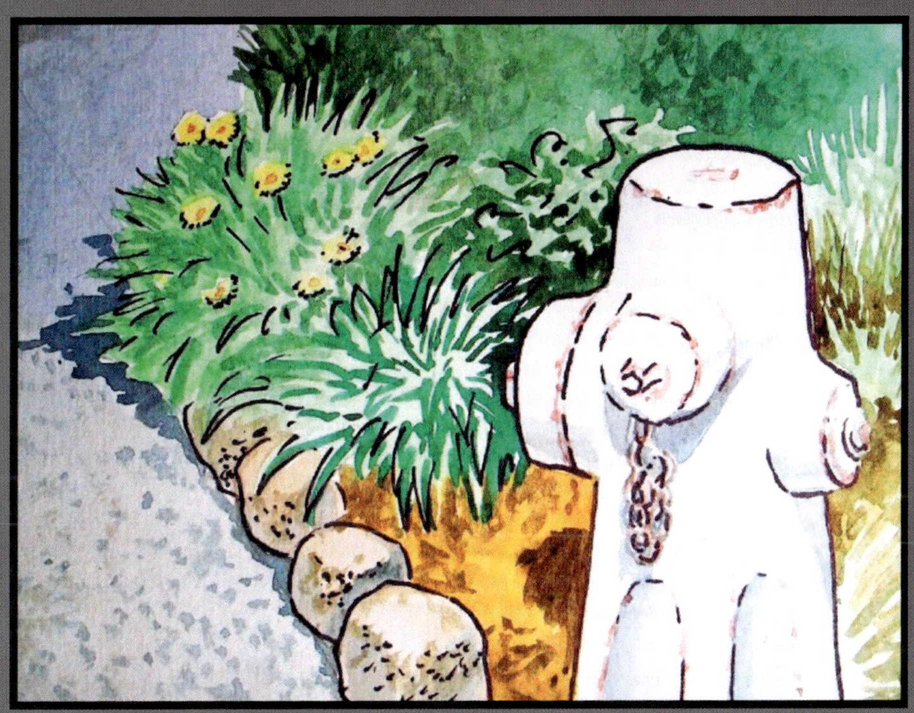

Down My Street

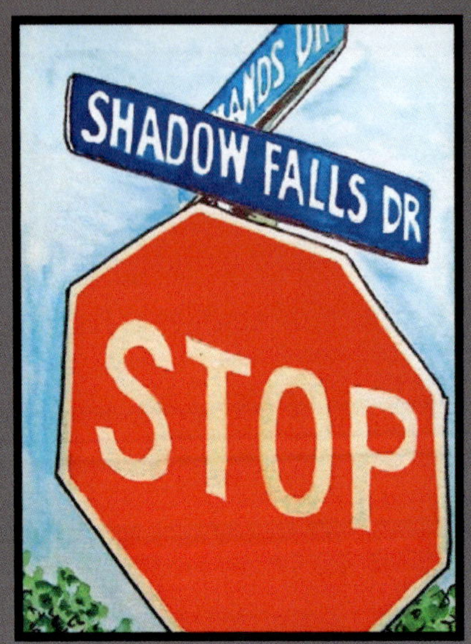

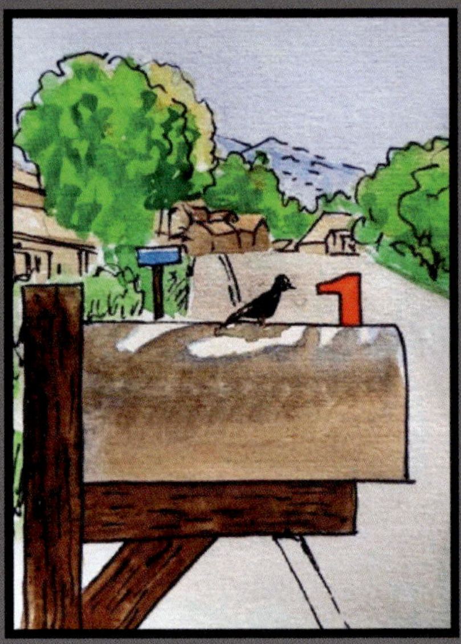

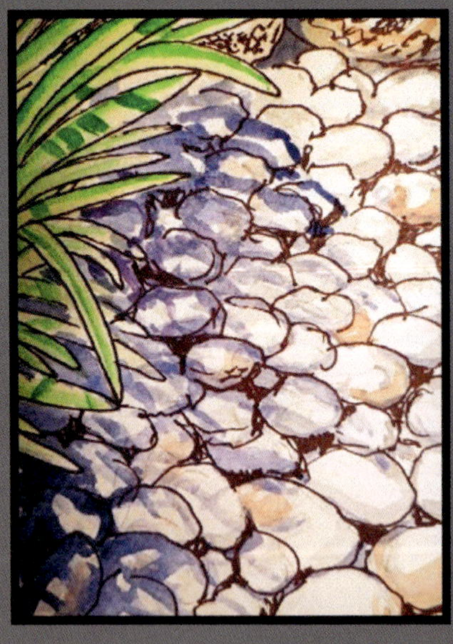

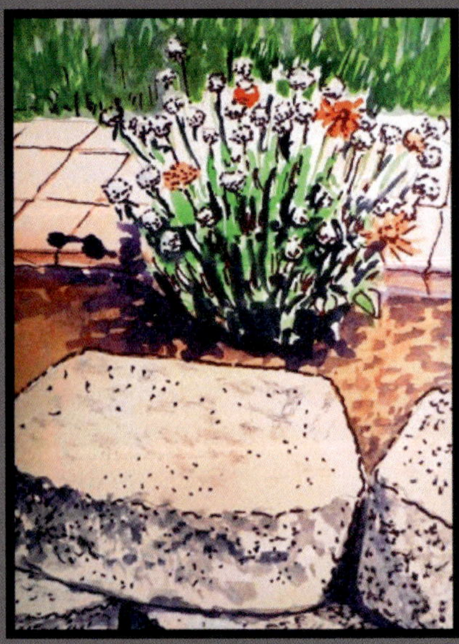

Down My Street

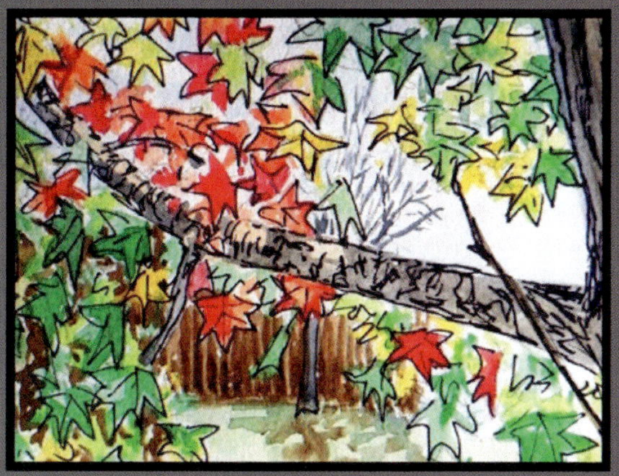

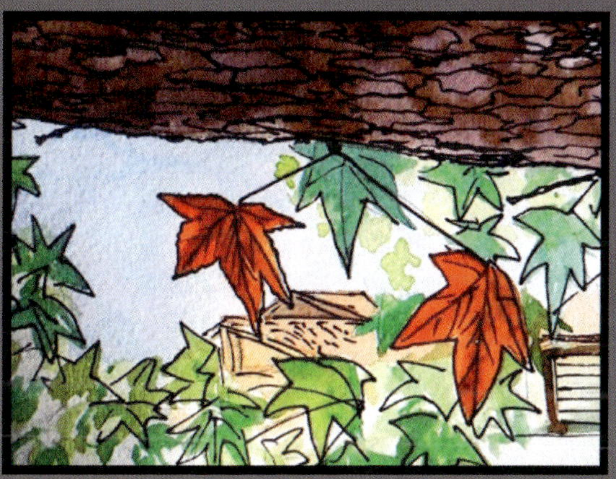

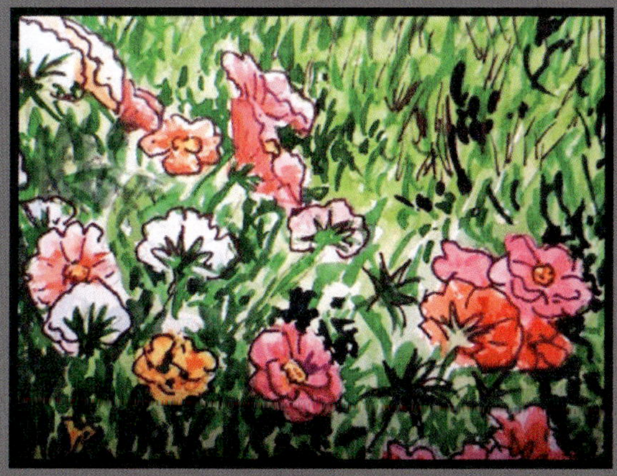

Down My Street

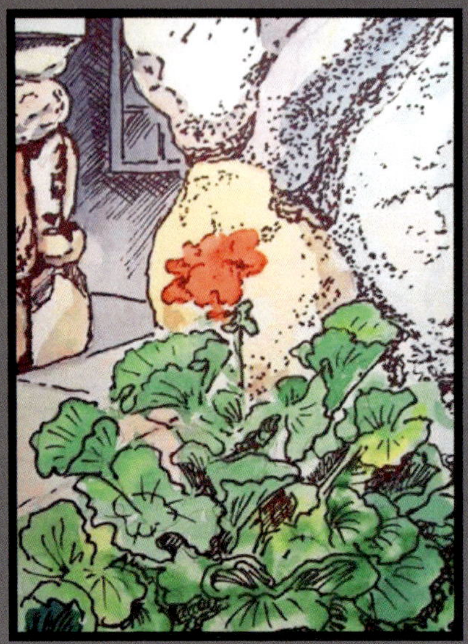
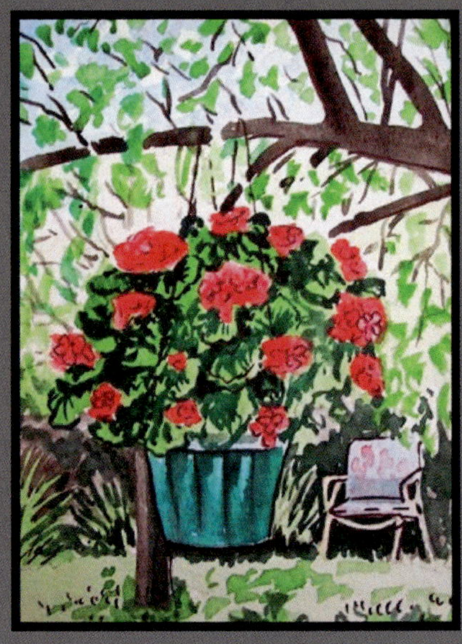

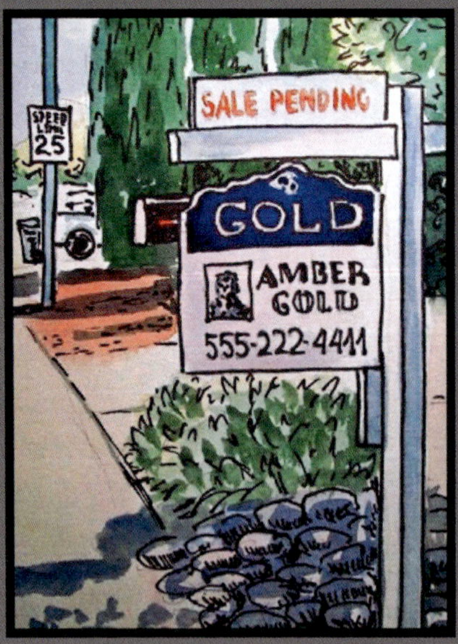

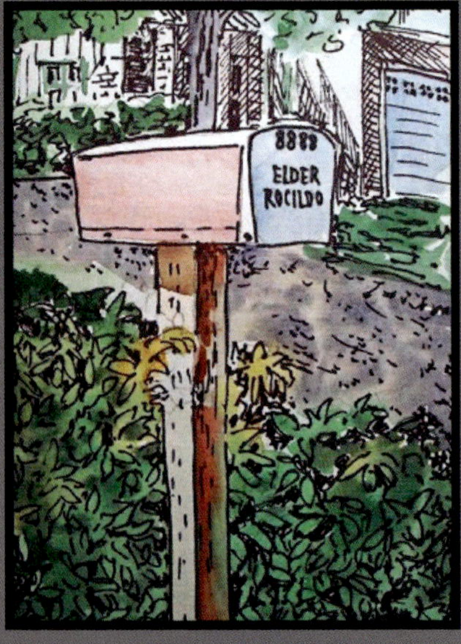

Down My Street

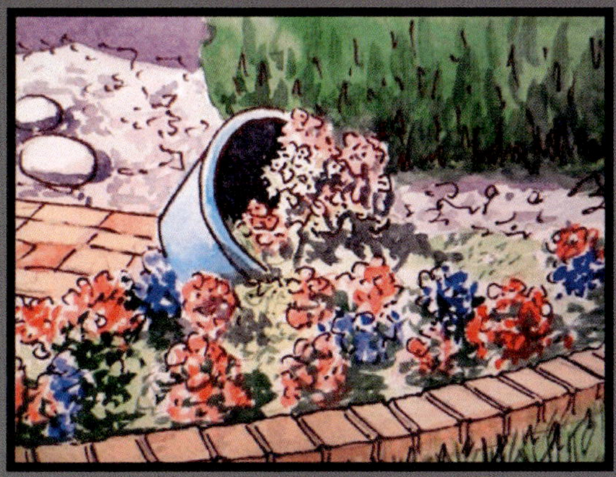

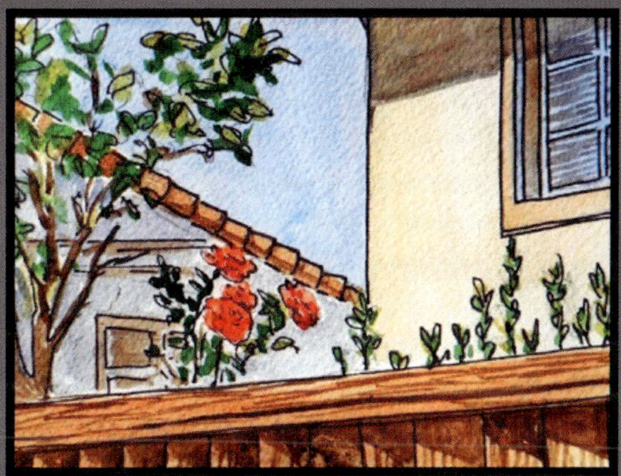

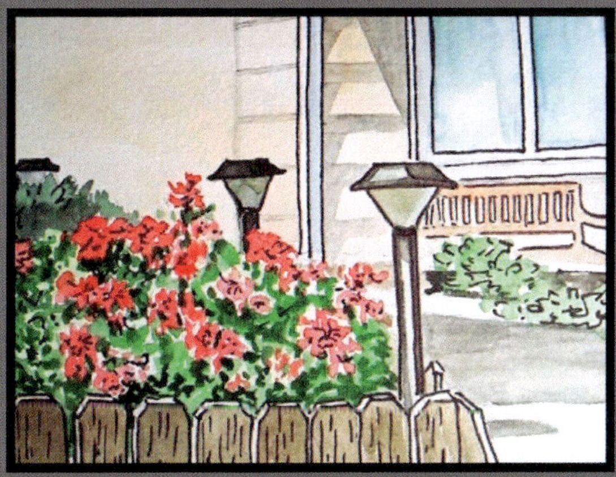

Down My Street

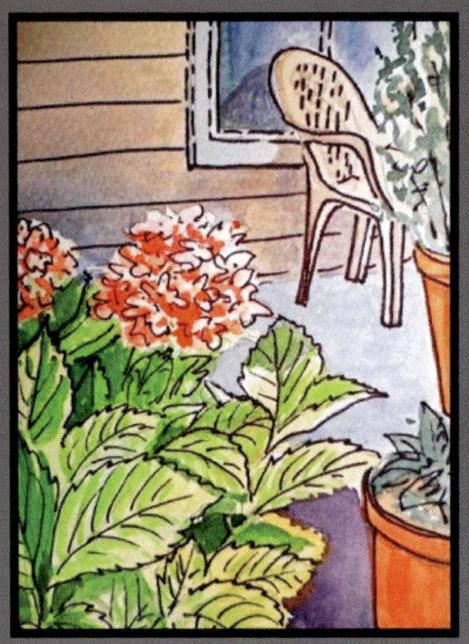
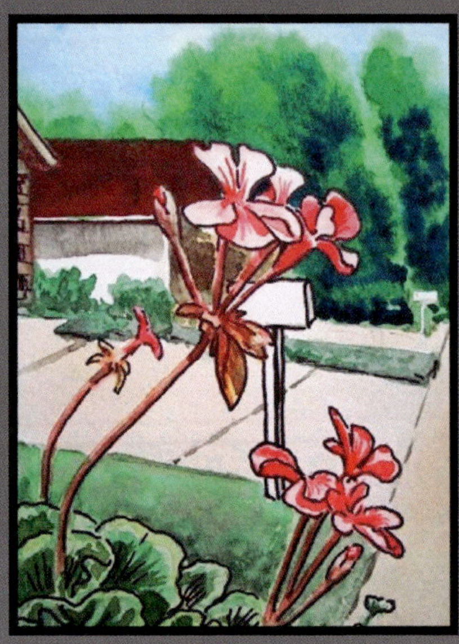
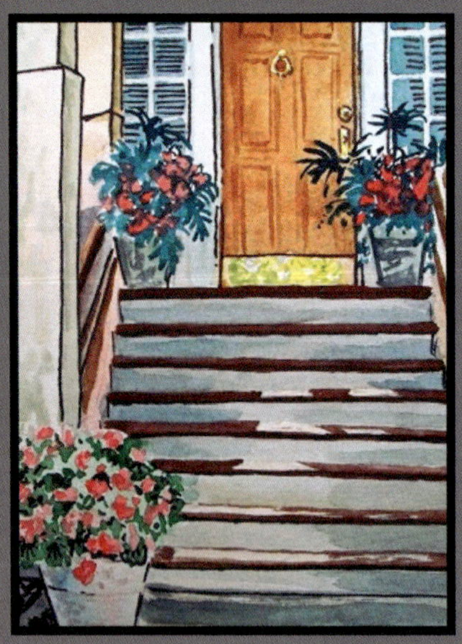
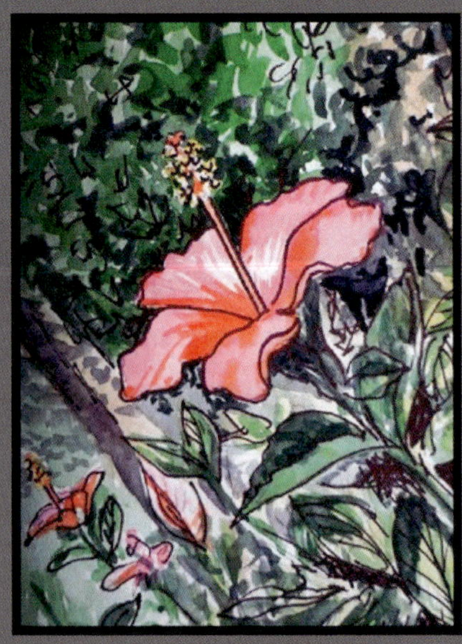

Down My Street

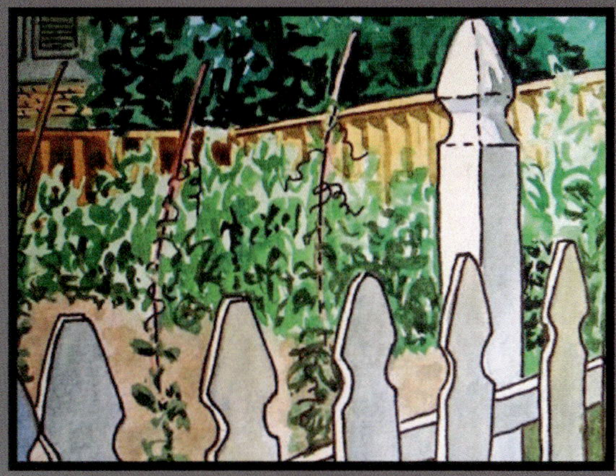

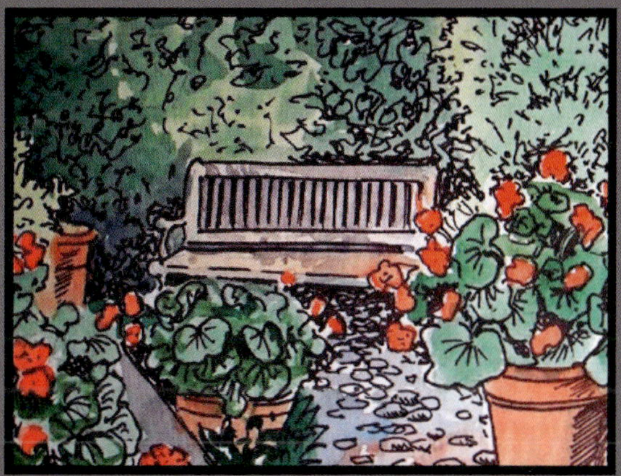

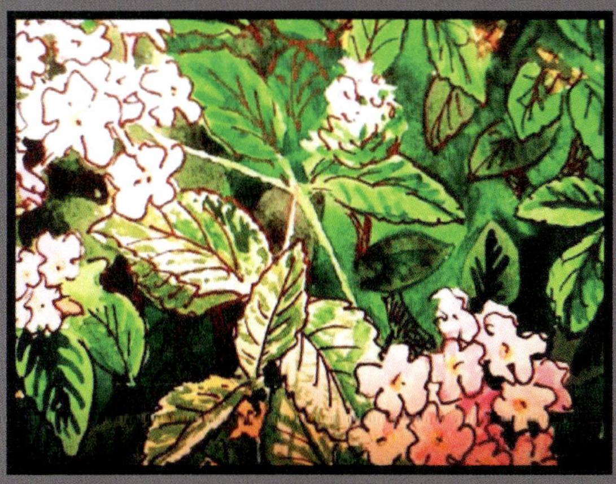

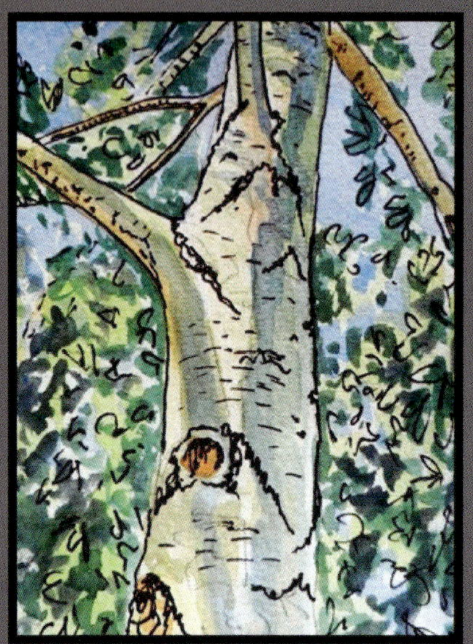
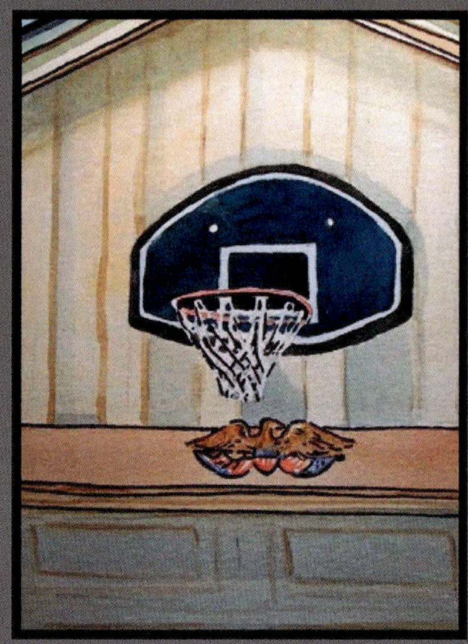

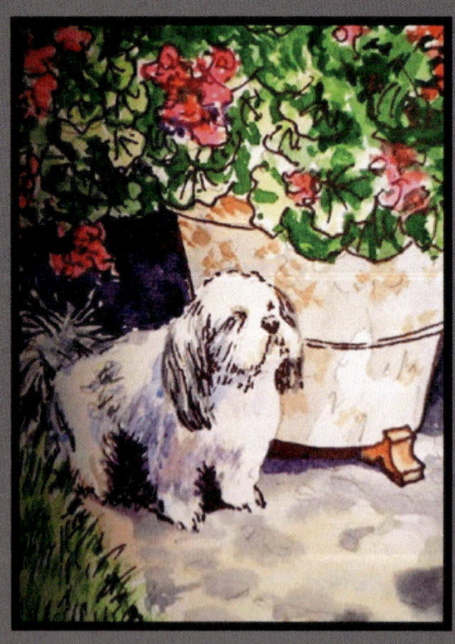
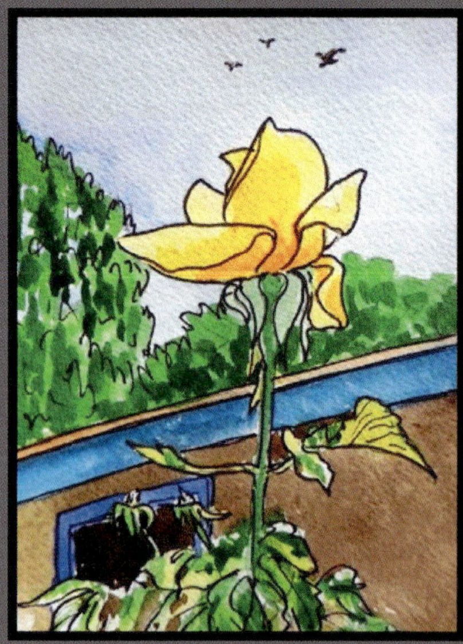

Down My Street

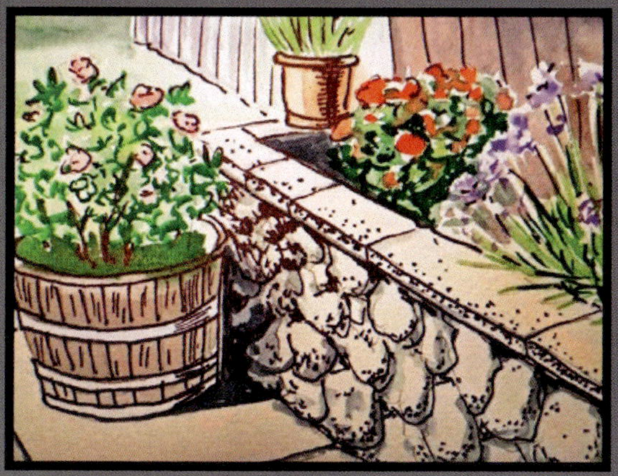

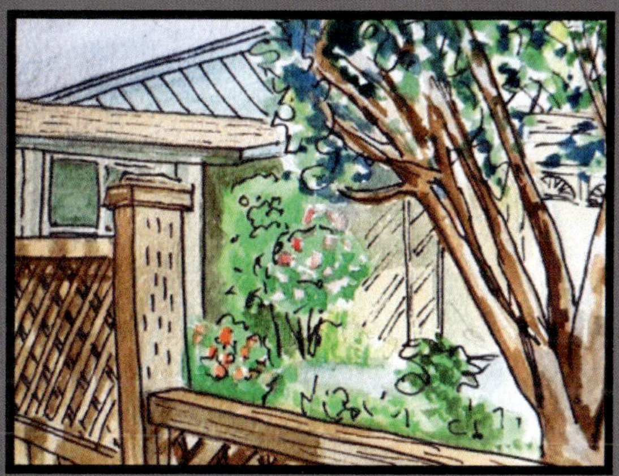

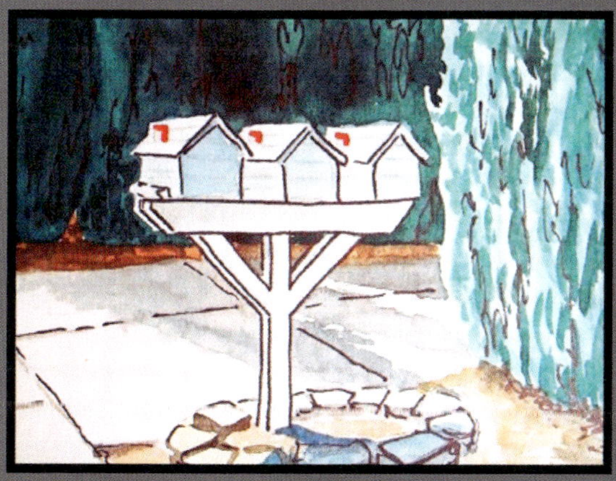

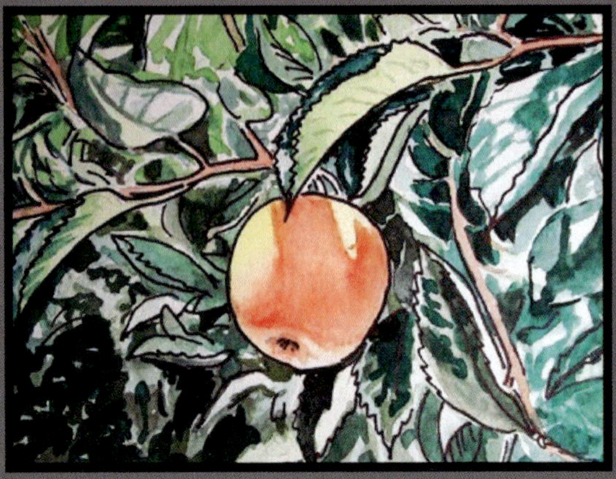

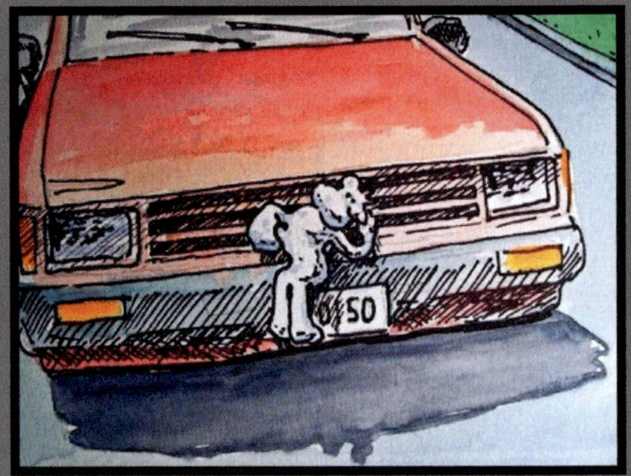

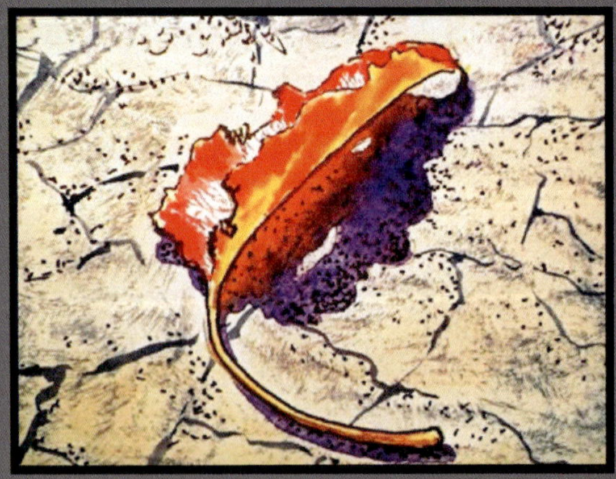

24447797R00016

Printed in Poland
by Amazon Fulfillment
Poland Sp. z o.o., Wrocław